Introduction to Data Science with Python

Basics of Numpy and Pandas

Mark Smart

Copyright©2018 Mark Smart
All Rights Reserved

Copyright © 2018 by Mark Smart

All rights reserved. No part of this publication may be reproduced, distributed, or transmitted in any form or by any means, including photocopying, recording, or other electronic or mechanical methods, without the prior written permission of the author, except in the case of brief quotations embodied in critical reviews and certain other noncommercial uses permitted by copyright law.

Tags: data science with python, python, pandas programming, numpy, pandas, pandas python, pandas in python, numpy in python, numpy python, numpy pandas, data science, ms excel books, json, python for data science, pivot tables, excel pivot tables, data visualisation, data visualisation python, data visualisation for dummies, data visualisation excel, algorithms for data science.

Table of Contents

Introduction   5

Chapter 1- Getting Started with Python for Data Science   6

Chapter 2- Working with Numpy   9

Chapter 3- Working with Pandas   19

Chapter 4- Cleansing Data   47

Chapter 5- Working with CSV Data   53

Chapter 6- Working with XLS Data   59

Chapter 7- Data Wrangling   67

Chapter 8- Measures of Central Tendency   72

Chapter 9- Calculating Variance   75

Chapter 10- Normal Distribution   78

Chapter 11- Working with JSON Data   80

Chapter 12- Data Visualization   82

Conclusion   100

Disclaimer

While all attempts have been made to verify the information provided in this book, the author does assume any responsibility for errors, omissions, or contrary interpretations of the subject matter contained within. The information provided in this book is for educational and entertainment purposes only. The reader is responsible for his or her own actions and the author does not accept any responsibilities for any liabilities or damages, real or perceived, resulting from the use of this information.

The trademarks that are used are without any consent, and the publication of the trademark is without permission or backing by the trademark owner. All trademarks and brands within this book are for clarifying purposes only and are the owned by the owners themselves, not affiliated with this document.

Introduction

Data is very essential for decision making. Data science involves the extraction of intelligence from data for decision making. The intelligence in this case can be trends, patterns, relationships etc. Companies generate data in huge amounts. This data is kept in various storages, both online and offline. The data is very rich and when analyzed properly, the company can gain insights that are good for decision making. However, analysis of such data is not easy when done manually. The best way to analyze data is by using automated means. Pandas and Numpy are libraries good for data analysis. The two libraries are packed with methods that can be used for data analysis. This book guides you on how to use these two libraries in Python for data analysis. Enjoy reading!

Chapter 1- Getting Started with Python for Data Science

Why Python for Data Science?

Python has gained a lot of interest as a good tool for data analysis. Python can be compared to tools such as SAS (Statistical Analysis Software) and R programming language. Python offers the following benefits:

1. It is open source, hence free to install.

2. Python is easy to learn.

3. It has an active and friendly online community.

4. It has the potential of becoming a common language for data science and for production of analytics products on the web.

However, note that Python is interpreted rather than being compiled. This means that it can take a lot of your CPU time. This doesn't make it a bad tool for data science since it is easy to learn Python. This will save you time.

What is Numpy?

Numpy stands for "Numeric Python" or "Numerical Python". It is a Python module (open source) that provides a faster way of doing mathematical computation on arrays and matrices. Arrays and matrices are very essential in most machine learning ecosystems, hence when Numpy is combined with other machine learning modules such as Scikit-learn, Matplotlib, TensorFlow, Pandas and others, the machine learning ecosystem becomes complete. Numpy simply introduces array-oriented computation functionalities. It can be imported as follows:

import numpy as np

The main object for Numpy is the homogenous multidimensional array, which is simply a table with elements of the same type, that is, integers, or characters or strings, but these are mostly integers. The dimensions are known as *axes*.

What is Pandas?

Just like Numpy, Pandas is another Python library popular for data science. It comes with easy to use, high performance structures and tools for data analysis.

We stated that Numpy provides objects for multi-dimensional arrays. Pandas instead provide in-memory 2d table object known as *DataFrame*. You can see this as a spreadsheet with both column names and row labels.

With the 2d tables, Pandas is capable of providing additional functionalities such as creation of pivot tables, plotting graphs and computing columns depending on other columns. We can import *Pandas* by running the following command:

import pandas as pd

The following are the common objects provided by the Pandas library:

1. Series objects- examples include 1D array, which is the same as a column in a spreadsheet.

2. DataFrame objects- an example of this is 2D table, which is the same as a spreadsheet.

3. Panel objects- this is a dictionary of DataFrame, which is the same as a sheet in MS Excel.

Chapter 2- Working with Numpy

You can first load the library and check for the version you are using:

import numpy as np
np.__version__

This returns the following in my case:

```
>>> import numpy as np
>>> np.__version__
'1.13.3'
>>>
```

You can then create a list with numbers 0 to 10 by running the following command:

L = list(range(11))

We should then convert the integers into a string, a process called *list comprehension*. This, we will be able to perform various operations to manipulate our list. The conversion can be done as follows:

[str(c) for c in L]

```
>>> [str(c) for c in L]
['0', '1', '2', '3', '4', '5', '6', '7', '8', '9', '10']
>>>
```

To return the types of the elements, run this command:

[type(item) for item in L]

```
>>> [type(item) for item in L]
[<class 'int'>, <class 'int'>, <class 'int'>, <class 'int'>, <class 'int'>, <cla
ss 'int'>, <class 'int'>, <class 'int'>, <class 'int'>, <class 'i
nt'>]
```

Creating Arrays

Numpy arrays are homogenous, that is, they can only store elements that belong to the same type. This is not the case with lists. We can create an array with 10 ones (1's) by running the following command:

np.ones(10, dtype='int')

```
>>> np.ones(10, dtype='int')
array([1, 1, 1, 1, 1, 1, 1, 1, 1, 1])
>>>
```

We can also create a 3 row x 5 column matrix with zeroes (0s) by running the following command:

np.zeros((3,5), dtype=float)

```
>>> np.zeros((3,5), dtype=float)
array([[ 0.,  0.,  0.,  0.,  0.],
       [ 0.,  0.,  0.,  0.,  0.],
       [ 0.,  0.,  0.,  0.,  0.]])
>>>
```

We can also create a matrix and predefine its value. This is shown below:

np.full((3,5),2.34)

```
>>> np.full((3,5),2.34)
array([[ 2.34,  2.34,  2.34,  2.34,  2.34],
       [ 2.34,  2.34,  2.34,  2.34,  2.34],
       [ 2.34,  2.34,  2.34,  2.34,  2.34]])
>>>
```

Above, we have created a 3 row by 5 column matrix with the value *2.34*.

We can also create an array with a sequence of items:

np.arange(0, 10, 2)

Above, we are creating an array with elements between 0 and 10 with a spacing of 2. The command will return the following:

```
>>> np.arange(0, 10, 2)
array([0, 2, 4, 6, 8])
>>>
```

We can create a 4 x 4 array with a mean of 0 and a standard deviation of 1:

np.random.normal(0, 1, (4,4))

```
>>> np.random.normal(0, 1, (4,4))
array([[ 0.47824984,  0.99994918, -0.18133351, -0.36427864],
       [ 0.28640797, -0.25600816, -1.98236812, -0.82844917],
       [ 0.8350854 , -0.01676583,  0.13228645,  1.40430639],
       [ 0.50266833,  0.158187  , -0.62739725, -1.28956122]])
>>>
```

An identity matrix can be created as follows:

np.eye(4)

```
>>> np.eye(4)
array([[ 1.,  0.,  0.,  0.],
       [ 0.,  1.,  0.,  0.],
       [ 0.,  0.,  1.,  0.],
       [ 0.,  0.,  0.,  1.]])
>>>
```

Array Indexing

Array elements in Python begins at index 0, meaning that the first element in the array is at index 0. Let us create a sample array and access the element stored at its index 0:

x1 = np.array([9, 8, 7, 4, 9, 4])
x1[0]

```
>>> x1 = np.array([9, 8, 7, 4, 9, 4])
>>> x1[0]
9
>>>
```

It returns 9, which is the first element in the array.

To access the third element of the array, we run the following command:

x1[4]

```
>>> x1[4]
9
>>> |
```

The last value of the array can be accessed with the -1 argument:

x1[-1]

```
>>> x1[-1]
4
>>>
```

The second last element can be accessed with -2 and this continues. Here is an example of creating a multi-dimensional array:

x2=np.array([[2, 9, 5, 5],[5, 1, 6, 9],[3, 7, 5, 9]])
x2[2,3]

This will return the following:

```
>>> x2=np.array([[2, 9, 5, 5],[5, 1, 6, 9],[3, 7, 5, 9]])
>>> x2[2,3]
9
```

The command returns the element at 1ˢᵗ row and 2ⁿᵈ column. The value at index 0, 0 can be replaced as follows:

x2[0,0] = 11

```
>>> x2
array([[11, 9, 5, 5],
       [ 5, 1, 6, 9],
       [ 3, 7, 5, 1]])
>>>
```

Array Slicing

Let us see how we may access multiple or a range of elements from an array. Consider the following:

x = np.arange(10)
x

```
>>> x = np.arange(10)
>>> x
array([0, 1, 2, 3, 4, 5, 6, 7, 8, 9])
>>>
```

The elements from the first to the 3ʳᵈ position can be accessed as follows:

x[:4]

```
>>> x[:4]
array([0, 1, 2, 3])
>>>
```

The elements from the 4th position to the end can be accessed as follows:

x[4:]

```
>>> x[4:]
array([4, 5, 6, 7, 8, 9])
>>>
```

The array can be reversed as follows:

x[::-1]

```
>>> x[::-1]
array([9, 8, 7, 6, 5, 4, 3, 2, 1, 0])
>>>
```

Array Concatenation

Sometimes, we may have to combine arrays. Instead of typing their elements individually, we can simply concatenate them. This is demonstrated below:

>>> x = np.array([1, 4, 5])
>>> y = np.array([3, 7, 9])
>>> z = [31,31,31]
>>> np.concatenate([x, y,z])

```
>>> x = np.array([1, 4, 5])
>>> y = np.array([3, 7, 9])
>>> z = [31,31,31]
>>> np.concatenate([x, y,z])
array([ 1,  4,  5,  3,  7,  9, 31, 31, 31])
>>>
```

We have created three arrays, x, y and z. We have then called the *concatenate()* function to concatenate them. The result we get is a concatenation of the values for the three arrays.

The *concatenate()* function may also be used for creating a 2-dimensional array:

grid = np.array([[1,4,7],[3,5,9]])
np.concatenate([grid,grid])

```
>>> grid = np.array([[1,4,7],[3,5,9]])
>>> np.concatenate([grid,grid])
array([[1, 4, 7],
       [3, 5, 9],
       [1, 4, 7],
       [3, 5, 9]])
>>>
```

It provides the *axis* parameter which can be used for defining a row-wise or column-wise matrix. So far, the concatenate function has been used to work on arrays of the same dimension. However, we may sometimes need to combine arrays of different dimensions, for example, 2D and 1D array.

In such a case, the use of *np.concatenate* function may not be appropriate. We can use the *np.vstack* or *np.hstack* function for this. Let us demonstrate this:

x = np.array([2,4,7])
grid = np.array([[3,2,9],[17,18,19]])
np.vstack([x,grid])

```
>>> x = np.array([2,4,7])
>>> grid = np.array([[3,2,9],[17,18,19]])
>>> np.vstack([x,grid])
array([[ 2,  4,  7],
       [ 3,  2,  9],
       [17, 18, 19]])
>>>
```

An array can also be added using *np.hstack*. This is demonstrated below:

z = np.array([[8],[8]])
np.hstack([grid,z])

```
>>> z = np.array([[8],[8]])
>>> np.hstack([grid,z])
array([[ 3,  2,  9,  8],
       [17, 18, 19,  8]])
>>>
```

Arrays can also be split based on some pre-defined positions. Let us begin by creating an array x:

x = np.arange(10)
x

```
>>> x = np.arange(10)
>>> x
array([0, 1, 2, 3, 4, 5, 6, 7, 8, 9])
>>>
```

Let us then split the array *x* into three arrays x1, x2 and x3:

x1,x2,x3 = np.split(x,[3,6])
print(x1,x2,x3)

```
>>> x1,x2,x3 = np.split(x,[3,6])
>>> print(x1,x2,x3)
[0 1 2] [3 4 5] [6 7 8 9]
>>>
```

The array has been split into 3 arrays. The first split is done at the third element, while the second one happens at the 6th element, resulting into three arrays.

Other than the functions we have discussed above, Numpy has several other functions that can be used for manipulation of data. We will discuss them later.

Chapter 3- Working with Pandas

Load the library by running the following command:

import pandas as pd

We have used pd as the alias.

Data Frames

We now need to create a data frame. Data frames store data in rectangular frames that can be viewed easily. We will use a dictionary in which keys will be converted into column named while values will be converted into row values:

import pandas as pd
import numpy as np

data = np.array([['','Column1','Column2'],['Row1',10, 20],['Row2',30,40]])

print(pd.DataFrame(data=data[1:,1:],index=data[1:,0],columns=data[0,1:]))

The code will return the following:

```
>>> import pandas as pd
>>> import numpy as np
>>> data = np.array([['','Column1','Column2'],['Row1',10,20],['Row2',30,40]])
>>> print(pd.DataFrame(data=data[1:,1:],index=data[1:,0],columns=data[0,1:]))
     Column1 Column2
Row1      10      20
Row2      30      40
>>>
```

Here is another example showing how we can create a data frame:

>>> **data = pd.DataFrame({'Country': ['Russia','Colombia','Chile','Equador','Nigeria'],**

       'Rank':[121,40,100,130,11]})
>>> **data**

The code will return the following:

```
>>> data = pd.DataFrame({'Country': ['Russia','Colombia','Chile','Equador','Nigeria'],
                         'Rank':[121,40,100,130,11]})
>>> data
    Country  Rank
0    Russia   121
1  Colombia    40
2     Chile   100
3   Equador   130
4   Nigeria    11
>>>
```

To get a summary of the data, run the following command:

data.describe()

```
>>> data.describe()
              Rank
count     5.000000
mean     80.400000
std      52.300096
min      11.000000
25%      40.000000
50%     100.000000
75%     121.000000
max     130.000000
>>>
```

The *describe()* method can only be used for computing the summary statistics for integer and double values. The *info()* function can help you get complete information about the entire set:

data.info()

```
>>> data.info()
<class 'pandas.core.frame.DataFrame'>
RangeIndex: 5 entries, 0 to 4
Data columns (total 2 columns):
Country    5 non-null object
Rank       5 non-null int64
dtypes: int64(1), object(1)
memory usage: 160.0+ bytes
>>>
```

Let us now create another data frame:

>>> data = pd.DataFrame({'group':['x', 'x', 'x', 'y','y', 'y', 'z', 'z','z'],'ounces':[5, 4, 11, 7, 8.5, 9, 3, 7, 6]})

>>> data

```
>>> data = pd.DataFrame({'group':['x', 'x', 'x', 'y','y', 'y', 'z', 'z','z'],'ou
nces':[5, 4, 11, 7, 8.5, 9, 3, 7, 6]})
>>> data
   group  ounces
0    x      5.0
1    x      4.0
2    x     11.0
3    y      7.0
4    y      8.5
5    y      9.0
6    z      3.0
7    z      7.0
8    z      6.0
>>>
```

Sorting Data

Let us now use the column for *ounces* to sort the data:

data.sort_values(by=['ounces'],ascending=True,inplace=False)

The data will be sorted as follows:

```
>>> data.sort_values(by=['ounces'],ascending=True,inplace=False)
   group  ounces
6    z      3.0
1    x      4.0
0    x      5.0
8    z      6.0
3    y      7.0
7    z      7.0
4    y      8.5
5    y      9.0
2    x     11.0
>>>
```

The parameter *inplace = True* makes changes to the data. We can also use multiple columns to sort the data. This is shown below:

data.sort_values(by=['group','ounces'],ascending=[True,False],inplace=False)

Above we have used both columns to sort the data, hence we get the following:

```
>>> data.sort_values(by=['group','ounces'],ascending=[True,False],inplace=False)
   group  ounces
2    x     11.0
0    x      5.0
1    x      4.0
5    y      9.0
4    y      8.5
3    y      7.0
7    z      7.0
8    z      6.0
6    z      3.0
>>>
```

Handling Outliers

In most cases, data has duplicate rows. This is noise, hence the need to clean it. This can be done as demonstrated below:

Let us create another data with duplicate rows:

data = pd.DataFrame({'x1':['one']*3 + ['two']*4, 'x2':[3, 2, 1, 3, 3, 4, 4]})

```
>>> data = pd.DataFrame({'x1':['one']*3 + ['two']*4, 'x2':[3, 2, 1, 3, 3, 4, 4]})
>>> data
    x1  x2
0  one   3
1  one   2
2  one   1
3  two   3
4  two   3
5  two   4
6  two   4
>>>
```

Let use the column x2 to sort the data:

data.sort_values(by='x2')

```
>>> data.sort_values(by='x2')
     x1  x2
2   one   1
1   one   2
0   one   3
3   two   3
4   two   3
5   two   4
6   two   4
>>>
```

We can then remove the duplicate data by calling the *drop_duplicates()* method:

data.drop_duplicates()

```
>>> data.drop_duplicates()
     x1  x2
0   one   3
1   one   2
2   one   1
3   two   3
5   two   4
>>>
```

The duplicates were removed by matching the row values across columns. Also, the duplicates can be removed by use of a column. Let us do away with all duplicates in the x1 column:

data.drop_duplicates(subset='x1')

```
>>> data.drop_duplicates(subset='x1')
    x1  x2
0  one   3
3  two   3
>>>
```

Rows can also be categorized depending on some pre-defined criteria. This is very essential during data processing as you may need to categorize variables. A good example of this is when we have a column with a list of countries and we need to create another column named "continent" which will be based on the "countries" column. This can be done as demonstrated below:

data = pd.DataFrame({'food': ['bacon', 'bacon', 'Pastrami','corned beef', 'pulled pork', 'Bacon', 'honey ham', 'pastrami', 'nova lox'],

'ounces': [3, 4, 11, 7, 9.5, 6, 2, 4, 8]})

```
>>> data = pd.DataFrame({'food': ['bacon', 'bacon', 'Pastrami','corned beef', 'p
ulled pork', 'Bacon', 'honey ham', 'pastrami', 'nova lox'],
             'ounces': [3, 4, 11, 7, 9.5, 6, 2, 4, 8]})
>>> data
          food  ounces
0        bacon     3.0
1        bacon     4.0
2     Pastrami    11.0
3  corned beef     7.0
4  pulled pork     9.5
5        Bacon     6.0
6    honey ham     2.0
7     pastrami     4.0
8     nova lox     8.0
>>>
```

We now need to create a new column for the name of the animal which is the source of each of the above. We should begin by creating a dictionary that will map each of the above foods to the right animal. The map function will then be used for mapping the values of the dictionary to the keys. This is shown below:

```
food_to_animal = {
      'bacon': 'pig',
'pulled pork': 'pig',
'pastrami': 'cow',
'corned beef': 'cow',
'honey ham': 'pig',
'nova lox': 'salmon'
      }
def food_2_animal(series):
   if series['food'] == 'bacon':
      return 'pig'
   elif series['food'] == 'pulled pork':
      return 'pig'
   elif series['food'] == 'pastrami':
      return 'cow'
   elif series['food'] == 'corned beef':
      return 'cow'
   elif series['food'] == 'honey ham':
      return 'pig'
   else:
      return 'salmon'
```

#creating a new variable

data['animal'] = data['food'].map(str.lower).map(food_to_animal)

data

```
>>> data = pd.DataFrame({'food': ['bacon', 'bacon', 'Pastrami','corned beef', 'p
ulled pork', 'Bacon', 'honey ham', 'pastrami', 'nova lox'],
                         'ounces': [3, 4, 11, 7, 9.5, 6, 2, 4, 8]})
>>> food_to_animal = {
        'bacon': 'pig',
    'pulled pork': 'pig',
    'pastrami': 'cow',
    'corned beef': 'cow',
    'honey ham': 'pig',
    'nova lox': 'salmon'
    }
>>> def food_2_animal(series):
    if series['food'] == 'bacon':
        return 'pig'
    elif series['food'] == 'pulled pork':
        return 'pig'
    elif series['food'] == 'pastrami':
        return 'cow'
    elif series['food'] == 'corned beef':
        return 'cow'
    elif series['food'] == 'honey ham':
        return 'pig'
    else:
        return 'salmon'
>>> data['animal'] = data['food'].map(str.lower).map(food_to_animal)
>>> data
          food  ounces  animal
0        bacon     3.0     pig
1        bacon     4.0     pig
2     Pastrami    11.0     cow
3  corned beef     7.0     cow
4  pulled pork     9.5     pig
5        Bacon     6.0     pig
6    honey ham     2.0     pig
7     pastrami     4.0     cow
8     nova lox     8.0  salmon
>>> |
```

The foods have now been mapped to the right animal.

We can also achieve the same by converting the food values into lower case then applying the function as shown below:

lower = lambda x: x.lower()

data['food'] = data['food'].apply(lower)

data['animal2'] = data.apply(food_2_animal, axis='columns')
data

This returns the following:

```
>>> lower = lambda x: x.lower()
>>> data['food'] = data['food'].apply(lower)
>>> data['animal2'] = data.apply(food_2_animal, axis='columns')
>>> data
         food  ounces  animal  animal2
0       bacon     3.0     pig      pig
1       bacon     4.0     pig      pig
2    pastrami    11.0     cow      cow
3  corned beef    7.0     cow      cow
4  pulled pork    9.5     pig      pig
5       bacon     6.0     pig      pig
6   honey ham     2.0     pig      pig
7    pastrami     4.0     cow      cow
8    nova lox     8.0  salmon   salmon
>>>
```

We can also use the *assign* function to create a new variable. New functions will help you know how powerful Pandas is:

data.assign(newVariable = data['ounces']*5)

This will multiply the values for *ounces* column with 5 and add the values into the *newvariable* column as shown below:

```
>>> data.assign(newVariable = data['ounces']*5)
        food  ounces  animal  animal2  newVariable
0      bacon     3.0     pig      pig         15.0
1      bacon     4.0     pig      pig         20.0
2   pastrami    11.0     cow      cow         55.0
3 corned beef    7.0     cow      cow         35.0
4 pulled pork    9.5     pig      pig         47.5
5      bacon     6.0     pig      pig         30.0
6  honey ham     2.0     pig      pig         10.0
7   pastrami     4.0     cow      cow         20.0
8   nova lox     8.0  salmon   salmon         40.0
>>>
```

If we don't need any of the columns in our data frame, we can drop it. Let us drop the column for *animal2*:

data.drop('animal2',axis='columns',inplace=True)
data

```
>>> data.drop('animal2',axis='columns',inplace=True)
>>> data
        food  ounces  animal
0      bacon     3.0     pig
1      bacon     4.0     pig
2   pastrami    11.0     cow
3 corned beef    7.0     cow
4 pulled pork    9.5     pig
5      bacon     6.0     pig
6  honey ham     2.0     pig
7   pastrami     4.0     cow
8   nova lox     8.0  salmon
>>>
```

Dealing with Missing Values

Most datasets have missing values. One of the quickest ways of handling this is by filling the missing value with a random number. Your dataset may also have numerous outliers which might need replacement. This can be handled easily in Pandas as we are going to demonstrate: let us begin by creating an array of data:

data = np.array([3., -799., 5., -799., -1000., 1.])
data

```
>>> data = np.array([3., -799., 5., -799., -1000., 1.])
>>> data
array([    3.,  -799.,     5.,  -799., -1000.,     1.])
>>>
```

Let us replace the -799 with NaN:

data.replace(-799, np.nan,inplace=True)

Renaming Columns

The names of columns in Pandas data frames can be renamed. Let us see how this can be done. Let us begin by creating a new data frame:

data = pd.DataFrame(np.arange(12).reshape((3, 4)),index=['USA', 'Canada', 'Russia'],columns=['a', 'b', 'c', 'd'])

data

This gives the following data frame:

```
>>> data = pd.DataFrame(np.arange(12).reshape((3, 4)),index=['USA', 'Canada', 'R
ussia'],columns=['a', 'b', 'c', 'd'])
>>> data
        a  b  c   d
USA     0  1  2   3
Canada  4  5  6   7
Russia  8  9  10  11
>>>
```

We can then call the *replace* function to replace the names of rows and columns that we need to change names:

data.rename(index = {'USA':'UK'}, columns={'a':'a_new','b':'b_new'},inplace=True)

data

This will return the following:

```
>>> data.rename(index = {'USA':'UK'}, columns={'a':'a_new','b':'b_new'},inplace=
True)
>>> data
        a_new  b_new  c   d
UK      0      1      2   3
Canada  4      5      6   7
Russia  8      9      10  11
>>>
```

The names for the countries can be changed to upper case by calling the *str* function:

**data.rename(index = str.upper, columns=str.title,inplace=True)
data**

```
>>> data.rename(index = str.upper, columns=str.title,inplace=True)
>>> data
        A_New  B_New   C   D
UK          0      1   2   3
CANADA      4      5   6   7
RUSSIA      8      9  10  11
>>>
```

Grouping Data

Pandas allows us to create groups and pivots on our data. Let us see how this can be used:

data = pd.DataFrame({'key1' : ['x', 'x', 'y', 'y', 'x'], 'key2' : ['one', 'two', 'one', 'two', 'one'], 'data1' : np.random.randn(5), 'data2' : np.random.randn(5)})

data

This will return the following data frame:

```
>>> data = pd.DataFrame({'key1' : ['x', 'x', 'y', 'y', 'x'], 'key2' : ['one', 't
wo', 'one', 'two', 'one'], 'data1' : np.random.randn(5), 'data2' : np.random.ran
dn(5)})
>>> data
      data1     data2 key1 key2
0  0.417068  1.204224    x  one
1  0.861676 -1.160010    x  two
2  1.432657 -0.587422    y  one
3 -0.683357 -1.255677    y  two
4 -0.939794 -0.673981    x  one
>>>
```

Let us group the values for column *data1* using *key2* column then get the mean:

group = data['data1'].groupby(data['key1'])

You will have grouped the data.

It is also possible for us to slice data frames in Pandas. Let us demonstrate this:

**dates = pd.date_range('20180807',periods=6)
data = pd.DataFrame(np.random.randn(6,4),index= dates,columns=list('ABCD'))**

data

This will return the following:

```
>>> dates = pd.date_range('20180807',periods=6)
>>> data = pd.DataFrame(np.random.randn(6,4),index=dates,columns=list('ABCD'))
>>> data
                   A         B         C         D
2018-08-07  1.275462  0.504645  0.431839  1.093544
2018-08-08  0.080306  0.075726 -0.636367 -0.031289
2018-08-09  0.568050 -1.419953  0.007687  0.479877
2018-08-10 -2.573195 -0.717867 -0.241909 -1.384918
2018-08-11  0.107976  0.261197  0.288745 -0.424963
2018-08-12  0.312650 -0.003743  1.345875  0.333782
>>>
```

To get the first three rows of the frame, we run the following command:

data[:3]

```
>>> data[:3]
                   A         B         C         D
2018-08-07  1.275462  0.504645  0.431839  1.093544
2018-08-08  0.080306  0.075726 -0.636367 -0.031289
2018-08-09  0.568050 -1.419953  0.007687  0.479877
>>>
```

The slicing can also be done by use of the data range as shown below:

df['20130807':'20130809']

We can also use the column names to do the slicing:

df.loc[:,['A','B']]

This will return the columns A and B as shown below:

```
>>> df.loc[:,['A','B']]
                   A         B
2013-01-01  1.206369  0.182912
2013-01-02  1.047675 -0.262104
2013-01-03  0.056688  0.963766
2013-01-04  1.912115  0.328292
2013-01-05  1.153415 -0.726294
2013-01-06 -0.128762  0.832805
>>>
```

A range of rows can be returned after running the following command:

df.iloc[2:4, 0:2]

```
>>> df.iloc[2:4, 0:2]
                   A         B
2013-01-03  0.056688  0.963766
2013-01-04  1.912115  0.328292
>>>
```

Anytime you need to copy a dataset, just call the *copy* method as shown below:

dff = df.copy()
dff

This will return the same data frame as shown below:

```
>>> dff = df.copy()
>>> dff
                   A         B         C         D
2013-01-01  1.206369  0.182912 -0.210550  2.059416
2013-01-02  1.047675 -0.262104  0.954832  1.821366
2013-01-03  0.056688  0.963766  1.492049  0.603433
2013-01-04  1.912115  0.328292 -0.797659 -0.930608
2013-01-05  1.153415 -0.726294 -0.286172  0.909583
2013-01-06 -0.128762  0.832805  0.775468 -1.138347
>>>
```

Our "*data*" data frame is as shown below:

```
>>> data
                   A         B         C         D
2018-08-07  1.275462  0.504645  0.431839  1.093544
2018-08-08  0.080306  0.075726 -0.636367 -0.031289
2018-08-09  0.568050 -1.419953  0.007687  0.479877
2018-08-10 -2.573195 -0.717867 -0.241909 -1.384918
2018-08-11  0.107976  0.261197  0.288745 -0.424963
2018-08-12  0.312650 -0.003743  1.345875  0.333782
>>> |
```

Let us add a new column E to it:

data['E']=['one', 'two','two','three','four','five']
data

The data frame will now be as follows:

```
>>> data['E']=['one', 'two','two','three','four','five']
>>> data
                   A         B         C         D      E
2018-08-07  1.275462  0.504645  0.431839  1.093544    one
2018-08-08  0.080306  0.075726 -0.636367 -0.031289    two
2018-08-09  0.568050 -1.419953  0.007687  0.479877    two
2018-08-10 -2.573195 -0.717867 -0.241909 -1.384918  three
2018-08-11  0.107976  0.261197  0.288745 -0.424963   four
2018-08-12  0.312650 -0.003743  1.345875  0.333782   five
>>>
```

We can select the data frame rows using the values of a particular column. Let us select the rows for which the values at column E are either *two* or *five*:

data[data['E'].isin(['two','five'])]

This returns the following rows:

```
>>> data[data['E'].isin(['two','five'])]
                   A         B         C         D     E
2018-08-08  0.080306  0.075726 -0.636367 -0.031289   two
2018-08-09  0.568050 -1.419953  0.007687  0.479877   two
2018-08-12  0.312650 -0.003743  1.345875  0.333782  five
>>>
```

If we need to choose all rows except the ones with two or five at column E, we can negate the above command as follows:

data[~data['E'].isin(['two','five'])]

```
>>> data[~data['E'].isin(['two','five'])]
                   A         B         C         D      E
2018-08-07  1.275462  0.504645  0.431839  1.093544    one
2018-08-10 -2.573195 -0.717867 -0.241909 -1.384918  three
2018-08-11  0.107976  0.261197  0.288745 -0.424963   four
>>>
```

Note that the negation has been done using the tilde (~).

The *query()* method can help us query our columns based on a specified criterion.

Suppose we need to get the rows in which the values of B are greater than the values of C. We can use the following command:

data.query('B > C')

```
>>> data.query('B > C')
                   A         B         C         D     E
2018-08-07  1.275462  0.504645  0.431839  1.093544   one
2018-08-08  0.080306  0.075726 -0.636367 -0.031289   two
>>>
```

We can also use the OR in our queries. They symbol for OR are |. It can be used as follows:

data.query('A < C | B > A')

In the above command, we are selecting rows in which the value of A is less than the value of C or the value of B is greater than the value of A. The command will return the following:

```
>>> data.query('A < C | B > A')
                   A         B         C         D      E
2018-08-10 -2.573195 -0.717867 -0.241909 -1.384918  three
2018-08-11  0.107976  0.261197  0.288745 -0.424963   four
2018-08-12  0.312650 -0.003743  1.345875  0.333782   five
>>>
```

37

Pivot Tables

Pivot tables help us analyze data by use of a customized tabular format. Pivot tables have made MS Excel popular. It provides us with an easy way of analyzing data.

Let us first create a new data frame:

**data = pd.DataFrame({'group': ['x', 'x', 'x', 'y','y', 'y', 'z', 'z','z'],
        'ounces': [3, 4, 10, 8, 9.1, 8, 4, 7, 9]})**

```
>>> data = pd.DataFrame({'group': ['x', 'x', 'x', 'y','y', 'y', 'z', 'z','z'],
        'ounces': [3, 4, 10, 8, 9.1, 8, 4, 7, 9]})
>>> data
  group  ounces
0   x     3.0
1   x     4.0
2   x    10.0
3   y     8.0
4   y     9.1
5   y     8.0
6   z     4.0
7   z     7.0
8   z     9.0
>>>
```

The following command can help us get the mean for every group of variables, that is, x, y and z:

data.pivot_table(values='ounces',index='group',aggfunc=np.mean)

```
>>> data.pivot_table(values='ounces',index='group',aggfunc=np.mean)
        ounces
group
x       5.666667
y       8.366667
z       6.666667
>>>
```

The above returns the mean for every group. Let us get the count for every group:

data.pivot_table(values='ounces',index='group',aggfunc='count')

```
>>> data.pivot_table(values='ounces',index='group',aggfunc='count')
        ounces
group
x       3
y       3
z       3
>>>
```

Exploring Large Datasets

You have known how to use Pandas to explore small datasets. Let us use it to explore large ones. We will use the adult dataset. In the dataset, *target* is the dependent variable. The dataset should be used in binary classification problems. Our goal is to be able to predict whether an individual has a salary of below or over 50K. Download the dataset and store it in the same directory as your python scripts. Let us now load it:

train = pd.read_csv("train.csv")

test = pd.read_csv("test.csv")

The dataset is now loaded. Ensure that you specify the path to the dataset correctly; otherwise you will get an error. You can then call the *info()* method to see details of the dataset:

train.info()

```
>>> train = pd.read_csv("train.csv")
>>> test = pd.read_csv("test.csv")
>>> train.info()
<class 'pandas.core.frame.DataFrame'>
RangeIndex: 32561 entries, 0 to 32560
Data columns (total 15 columns):
age               32561 non-null int64
workclass         30725 non-null object
fnlwgt            32561 non-null int64
education         32561 non-null object
education.num     32561 non-null int64
marital.status    32561 non-null object
occupation        30718 non-null object
relationship      32561 non-null object
race              32561 non-null object
sex               32561 non-null object
capital.gain      32561 non-null int64
capital.loss      32561 non-null int64
hours.per.week    32561 non-null int64
native.country    31978 non-null object
target            32561 non-null object
dtypes: int64(6), object(9)
memory usage: 3.7+ MB
>>>
```

The train dataset has 15 columns and 32561 rows. 6 of the 15 columns have integer classes while the rest have character or object classes. Here is a quick way of checking the row and column details for the dataset:

print ("The train dataset has",train.shape)
print ("The test dataset has",test.shape)

This returns the following result:

```
>>> print ("The train dataset has",train.shape)
The train dataset has (32561, 15)
>>> print ("The test dataset has",test.shape)
The test dataset has (16281, 15)
>>>
```

Let us see what the dataset has:

train.head()

```
>>> train.head()
    age        workclass   fnlwgt   education  education.num  \
0    39        State-gov    77516   Bachelors             13
1    50 Self-emp-not-inc    83311   Bachelors             13
2    38          Private   215646     HS-grad              9
3    53          Private   234721        11th              7
4    28          Private   338409   Bachelors             13

       marital.status         occupation   relationship    race     sex
0       Never-married       Adm-clerical  Not-in-family   White    Male
1  Married-civ-spouse    Exec-managerial        Husband   White    Male
2            Divorced  Handlers-cleaners  Not-in-family   White    Male
3  Married-civ-spouse  Handlers-cleaners        Husband   Black    Male
4  Married-civ-spouse     Prof-specialty           Wife   Black  Female

   capital.gain  capital.loss  hours.per.week  native.country  target
0          2174             0              40   United-States   <=50K
1             0             0              13   United-States   <=50K
2             0             0              40   United-States   <=50K
3             0             0              40   United-States   <=50K
4             0             0              40            Cuba   <=50K
>>>
```

Let us check whether our data has missing values:

nans = train.shape[0] - train.dropna().shape[0]

print ("%d rows in the train data have missing values " %nans)

```
>>> nans = train.shape[0] - train.dropna().shape[0]
>>> print ("%d rows in the train data have missing values " %nans)
2399 rows in the train data have missing values
>>>
```

You have the result above. Let us check the same for the test data:

**nand = test.shape[0] - test.dropna().shape[0]
print ("%d rows in the test data have missing values " %nand)**

```
>>> nand = test.shape[0] - test.dropna().shape[0]
>>> print ("%d rows in the test data have missing values " %nand)
1221 rows in the test data have missing values
>>>
```

We can now count the number of unique values in the character variables:

**cat = train.select_dtypes(include=['O'])
cat.apply(pd.Series.nunique)**

The missing values fall in all the three character variables. Let us impute the missing values with their corresponding modes:

For Education:

train.workclass.value_counts(sort=True)

train.workclass.fillna('Private',inplace=True)

For Occupation:

train.occupation.value_counts(sort=True)
train.occupation.fillna('Prof-specialty',inplace=True)

For Native Country:

train['native.country'].value_counts(sort=True)
train['native.country'].fillna('United-States',inplace=True)

You can then run the following command to see whether there is any missing value:

train.isnull().sum()

Let us now check our target variable to determine whether the data is imbalanced or not: we are checking the proportion of the target variable:

train.target.value_counts()/train.shape[0]

In my case, 75% of the data is below the <=50K class. What does this mean? Even after taking a rough guess of target prediction as <=50K, we will get an accuracy of 75%.

That is really exciting. Let us now create a cross tab for the target variable with education. This way, we will be able to tell the effect of education on our target variable:

pd.crosstab(train.education, train.target,margins=True)/train.shape[0]

```
>>> pd.crosstab(train.education, train.target,margins=True)/train.shape[0]
target         <=50K      >50K       All
education
10th           0.026750   0.001904   0.028654
11th           0.034243   0.001843   0.036086
12th           0.012285   0.001013   0.013298
1st-4th        0.004975   0.000184   0.005160
5th-6th        0.009736   0.000491   0.010227
7th-8th        0.018611   0.001228   0.019840
9th            0.014957   0.000829   0.015786
Assoc-acdm     0.024631   0.008139   0.032769
Assoc-voc      0.031357   0.011087   0.042443
Bachelors      0.096250   0.068210   0.164461
Doctorate      0.003286   0.009398   0.012684
HS-grad        0.271060   0.051442   0.322502
Masters        0.023464   0.029452   0.052916
Preschool      0.001566   0.000000   0.001566
Prof-school    0.004699   0.012991   0.017690
Some-college   0.181321   0.042597   0.223918
All            0.759190   0.240810   1.000000
>>>
```

The data shows that of all the 75% earning a salary of <=50K, 27% of them are high school graduates. This is correct since people with low level of education are paid less. Also, of the 25% of people with a salary of >=50K, 6% of them a bachelors while 5% of them are high school graduates.

Series

A series refers to a one-dimensional labeled array that can hold data of any type, including integer, double, character etc. The labels for the axis are collectively referred to as *index*. A Series is created using the constructor given below:

pandas.Series(data, index, dtype, copy)

Let us demonstrate how a series can be created from a Numpy array:

```
#import the libraries
import pandas as pd
import numpy as np
arr = np.array(['w','x','y','z'])
ser = pd.Series(arr)
print(ser)
```

Panel

A panel is simply a 3D container for data. Pandas allows us to create a panel using the following constructor:

pandas.Panel(data, items, major_axis, minor_axis, dtype, copy)

Let us demonstrate how a panel can be created with Pandas:

import pandas as pd
import numpy as np

data = {'df1' : pd.DataFrame(np.random.randn(4, 3)), 'df2' : pd.DataFrame(np.random.randn(4, 2))}
panel = pd.Panel(data)
print(panel)

First, we created a dictionary with two data frames. Each data frame holds a set of random numbers. We have then called the *Panel()* function and passed to it the name of the dictionary as the argument. It is expected to create a panel from this; the code gives the following result after execution:

```
<class 'pandas.core.panel.Panel'>
Dimensions: 2 (items) x 4 (major_axis) x 3 (minor_axis)
Items axis: df1 to df2
Major_axis axis: 0 to 3
Minor_axis axis: 0 to 2
```

Chapter 4- Cleansing Data

Data from the world has missing values. Machine learning models give a poor accuracy as a result of poor quality data that is brought about by missing values. We previously discussed how to handle missing values, but we did this shallowly. We now want to dig deep into this. Let us begin by creating a data frame with missing values:

import pandas as pd
import numpy as np

data = pd.DataFrame(np.random.randn(5, 3), index=['s', 'u', 'w', 'x',

'z'],columns=['one', 'two', 'three'])

data = data.reindex(['s', 't', 'u', 'v', 'w', 'x', 'y', 'z'])

print(data)

The code returns the following data frame:

```
        one       two     three
s  -0.654019  1.186528  0.145168
t        NaN       NaN       NaN
u   3.097401  0.769431 -0.614087
v        NaN       NaN       NaN
w  -0.536965  0.566882  0.365191
x  -0.495973 -0.539505 -1.010129
y        NaN       NaN       NaN
z  -0.450687  0.382741 -0.998844
>>>
```

NaN simply stands for *Not a Number*.

Checking for Missing Values

Pandas provides the *isnull()* and *notnull()* function that makes it easy to detect missing values. These methods can be applied on DataFrame and Series objects. Let us see how these methods can be used:

import pandas as pd
import numpy as np

data = pd.DataFrame(np.random.randn(5, 3), index=['s', 'u', 'w', 'x',

'z'],columns=['one', 'two', 'three'])

data = data.reindex(['s', 't', 'u', 'v', 'w', 'x', 'y', 'z'])

print(data['one'].isnull().sum())

This returns the following result:

```
3
>>>
```

This shows the number of missing values that we have.

Cleaning Missing Data

There are various methods provided by the Pandas library that can help in cleaning missing data. This can be done using the *fillna* method which fills the NA values with non-null data in different ways. Let us discuss these ways:

Replacing with a Scalar Value

Let us demonstrate how NaN can be replaced with a 0:

```
import pandas as pd
import numpy as np

data = pd.DataFrame(np.random.randn(3, 3),
index=['v', 'x', 'z'],columns=['one',

'two', 'three'])
data = data.reindex(['x', 'y', 'z'])
print(data)
print ("After replacing NaN with '0':")
print(data.fillna(0))
```

The code will print the following when executed:

```
          one       two     three
x    1.641769  0.347929 -0.342177
y         NaN       NaN       NaN
z   -0.029021  0.899601  1.055450
After replacing NaN with '0':
          one       two     three
x    1.641769  0.347929 -0.342177
y    0.000000  0.000000  0.000000
z   -0.029021  0.899601  1.055450
>>>
```

We have first generated a 3 by 3 data frame. This data frame has some NaN values. We have then replaced the NaN values with a 0. Note that you can fill it with any other value you need other than 0.

Fill Na

This can be used with the following methods:

1. pad/fill- Fill methods Forward.
2. bfill/backfill- Fill methods Backward.

Consider the example given below:

**import pandas as pd
import numpy as np**

data = pd.DataFrame(np.random.randn(5, 3), index=['s', 'u', 'w', 'x',

'y'],columns=['one', 'two', 'three'])

```
data = data.reindex(['s', 't', 'u', 'v', 'w', 'x', 'y', 'z'])

print(data.fillna(method='pad'))
```

The code will generate the following result:

```
        one       two      three
s   1.157859 -0.593488 -0.256053
t   1.157859 -0.593488 -0.256053
u   0.196948 -0.469346  0.556310
v   0.196948 -0.469346  0.556310
w   1.622259 -0.552031  0.320702
x  -1.674387 -1.056466  0.197428
y   0.985025 -0.101418  0.222024
z   0.985025 -0.101418  0.222024
>>>
```

Dropping Missing Values

If you need to drop the missing values, you can use the *dropna* method then pass the *axis* argument to it. BY default, the axis=0, along row, meaning that if there is any value within a row with a value of NA, then the entire row will excluded. Here is an example:

```
import pandas as pd
import numpy as np

data = pd.DataFrame(np.random.randn(5, 3), index=['s', 'u', 'w', 'x',

'z'],columns=['one', 'two', 'three'])
```

```
data = data.reindex(['s', 't', 'u', 'v', 'w', 'x', 'y', 'z'])
print(data.dropna())
```

The code will print the following:

```
        one       two     three
s  -0.467200  0.825245  1.022954
u  -0.157601  0.889543  0.754294
w  -1.360680 -0.563024 -0.214606
x  -0.678700 -0.186789  1.588883
z   0.445273  0.467884  0.604967
>>>
```

Replacing Missing/Generic Values

In some case, generic values should be replaced with specific values. The *replace* method can help us achieve this. The replacement of NA with a scalar value is similar to the behavior exhibited by the *fillna()* method. Consider the example given below:

```
import pandas as pd
import numpy as np
data = pd.DataFrame({'one':[10,20,30,40,50,2000],
'two':[1000,0,30,40,50,60]})
print(data.replace({1000:10,2000:60}))
```

The code will return the following result:

```
   one  two
0   10   10
1   20    0
2   30   30
3   40   40
4   50   50
5   60   60
>>>
```

Chapter 5- Working with CSV Data

CSV stands for Comma Separated Values. In data science, we always need to read CSV values. The reason is that we normally get our data from different sources. The Pandas library provides us with a way of reading CSV values, either in part or in whole. Let us discuss how this can be done:

Creating the CSV File

A csv file is simply a text file in which the values in different columns are separated using a comma (,). I have the following comma separated values:

id,surname,wage,start_date,dept
1,John,656.3,2014-03-02,Finance
2,Mercy,498.2,2015-08-21,Operations
3,Kogan,711,2014-11-15,ICT
4,Milly,729,2016-05-12,HR
5,Gary,856.21,2015-03-22,Finance
6,Pendo,578,2014-06-21,ICT
7,Michael,488.8,2014-07-28,Operations
8,Gerald,622.5,2013-06-16,HR

Just copy and save them with the name *employees.csv*. You only have to paste them in your notepad then save them in the directory where you save you Python scripts.

Reading the CSV File

The Pandas library provides us with the *read_csv* method that helps us read the contents of a csv file into the Python environment as a pandas DataFrame. For the method to read the file, you must pass the correct path to the file to it as the argument. This is demonstrated below:

import pandas as pd
data = pd.read_csv('employees.csv')
print(data)

In this case, I have simply passed the name of the file to the method. Why? It is because the file and Python script have been saved in the same directory. If I pass it as shown above, the Python interpreter will simply look for the file within the directory the script has been saved. If it is found, the data should be printed. If not found, the interpreter will return an error. In my case, the code prints the data on the Python terminal as shown below:

```
     id  surname    wage  start_date        dept
0    1     John   656.30  2014-03-02     Finance
1    2    Mercy   498.20  2015-08-21  Operations
2    3    Kogan   711.00  2014-11-15         ICT
3    4    Milly   729.00  2016-05-12          HR
4    5     Gary   856.21  2015-03-22     Finance
5    6    Pendo   578.00  2014-06-21         ICT
6    7  Michael   488.80  2014-07-28  Operations
7    8   Gerald   622.50  2013-06-16          HR
>>>
```

The file is exactly as it is. Its values have been organized into rows and columns, meaning that the Python interpreter as able to do this. However, don't forget that an additional column for indexes has been created, with the indexes begin at 0.

Reading Specific Rows

Sometimes, we may need to be specific and select only certain rows that meet the selection criterion. If we need, we can specify the column for which rows we need to select. Consider the example given below:

import pandas as pd
data = pd.read_csv('employees.csv')

 # Get the first 5 rows of the data
print (data[0:5]['wage'])

The code should return the first 5 rows of the *wage* column. Alternatively, this can be done by use of the *.loc()* method as shown below:

import pandas as pd
data = pd.read_csv('employees.csv')

 # Using the multi-axes indexing method
print (data.loc[[0,1,2,3,4,5],['wage']])

The code will return the following after execution:

```
     wage
0  656.30
1  498.20
2  711.00
3  729.00
4  856.21
5  578.00
>>>
```

Reading Specific Columns

The *read_csv* methid can also be used for reading some specific columns. This is achieved by using the multi-axes indexing method known as *.loc()*. Consider the example given below:

import pandas as pd
data = pd.read_csv('employees.csv')

 # Using the multi-axes indexing funtion
print (data.loc[:,['wage','surname']])

In the above code, we are reading the values for two columns, namely, the *age* and *surname* columns. When executed, the code returns the following:

```
     wage   surname
0  656.30      John
1  498.20     Mercy
2  711.00     Kogan
3  729.00     Milly
4  856.21      Gary
5  578.00     Pendo
6  488.80   Michael
7  622.50    Gerald
>>>
```

The above figure clearly shows that the code successfully extracted the two specified columns from our csv file.

Reading specified Rows and columns

It is possible for us to choose some columns for specified rows. This can be done with the *read_csv* function. The multi-axes indexing method *.loc()* can help us achieve this. Let us demonstrate how this can be done:

import pandas as pd
data = pd.read_csv('employees.csv')

 # Using the multi-axes indexing method
print (data.loc[[1,3,5],['wage','surname']])

What we are doing is that we are selecting the rows at indexes 1, 3 and 5. Note that indexes begin at 0, meaning the item at index 1 is in the second row. After choosing the rows, we are not to output all their columns, but only two of them, namely *wage* and *surname* columns. The code will return the following after execution:

```
   wage  surname
1  498.2   Mercy
3  729.0   Milly
5  578.0   Pendo
>>>
```

Reading a Range

We can use the *read_csv* function of the Pandas library to read certain columns and a range of rows. This is achieved via the *.loc()* method, which is a multi-axes indexing method. Consider the example given below:

**import pandas as pd
data = pd.read_csv('employees.csv')**

**# Using the multi-axes indexing method
print (data.loc[1:5,['wage','surname']])**

In the above code, we are selecting the *wage* and *surname* column for the rows in the range of index 1 to 5. Once the code is executed, it prints the following result:

```
     wage  surname
1  498.20    Mercy
2  711.00    Kogan
3  729.00    Milly
4  856.21     Gary
5  578.00    Pendo
>>>
```

Chapter 6- Working with XLS Data

MS Excel is a very popular problem. It has numerous appealing features which makes it a suitable tool in data science. The Pandas library provides us with a way of reading data stored in excel files and perform various operations on it. We can select the entire data or just part of it. The *read_excel* function is used for this purpose.

Let us demonstrate how this can be done.

Creating the Excel File

We will create an excel file with two sheets as shown below:

Sheet 1 should have the following data:

id,surname,wage,start_date,dept
1,John,656.3,2014-03-02,Finance
2,Mercy,498.2,2015-08-21,Operations
3,Kogan,711,2014-11-15,ICT
4,Milly,729,2016-05-12,HR
5,Gary,856.21,2015-03-22,Finance
6,Pendo,578,2014-06-21,ICT
7,Michael,488.8,2014-07-28,Operations
8,Gerald,622.5,2013-06-16,HR

Sheet 2 should have the following data:

Id	name	zipcode
1	john	3456
2	mercy	8976
3	kogan	5436
4	milly	8967
5	gary	9087
6	pendo	7823
7	michael	6734
8	gerald	4563

	A	B	C	D
1	id	name	zipcode	
2	1	john	3456	
3	2	mercy	8976	
4	3	kogan	5436	
5	4	milly	8967	
6	5	gary	9087	
7	6	pendo	7823	
8	7	michael	6734	
9	8	gerald	4563	

Reading the Excel File

We can use the *read_excel* function of the Pandas library to read the contents of an Excel file into the Python environment in the form of a data frame. We only have to specify the correct path to the file on the OS. The default setting is that the function reads Sheet1 of the Excel file.

Make sure that you have saved the Excel file as *employees.xlsx* and in the directory where you save your Python scripts. Write the following Python script:

import pandas as pd
data = pd.read_excel('employees.xlsx')
print (data)

we have called the *read_excel* function and passed the name of the file to read as the argument. The code will print the following when executed:

```
       id,surname,wage,start_date,dept
0           1,John,656.3,2014-03-02,Finance
1        2,Mercy,498.2,2015-08-21,Operations
2             3,Kogan,711,2014-11-15,ICT
3              4,Milly,729,2016-05-12,HR
4         5,Gary,856.21,2015-03-22,Finance
5              6,Pendo,578,2014-06-21,ICT
6    7,Michael,488.8,2014-07-28,Operations
7           8,Gerald,622.5,2013-06-16,HR
>>>
```

I initially had the problem of the *xlrd* module. The following error was generated:

ImportError: No module named 'xlrd'

However, I used pip3 to install the module by running the following command on the command prompt:

pip3 install xlrd

The module was installed and the con executed successfully. If you experience the same challenge, just do the same and the error will be solved? Note that the data has been read in the structure we saved it with. An additional column has been added showing the index for each row. Note this: We earlier stated that the code will read Sheet1 by default. What if we wanted it to read Sheet2? We could have modified our code to the following:

**import pandas as pd
data = pd.read_excel('employees.xlsx','Sheet2')
print (data)**

Upon execution, the code returns the following result:

```
   id    name  zipcode
0   1    john     3456
1   2   mercy     8976
2   3   kogan     5436
3   4   milly     8967
4   5    gary     9087
5   6   pendo     7823
6   7 michael     6734
7   8  gerald     4563
>>>
```

Reading Specific Rows and Columns

We can use the *read_excel* function to read some specific rows and columns in our excel file.

This can be accomplished via the *.loc()* method, which is a multi-axes indexing method. Consider the following example:

import pandas as pd
data = pd.read_excel('employees.xlsx','Sheet2')

 # Using the multi-axes indexing method
print (data.loc[[1,3,5],['name','zipcode']])

The code generates the following result after execution:

```
    name   zipcode
1   mercy    8976
3   milly    8967
5   pendo    7823
```

We have chosen to select only the *name* and *zipcode* columns from the second sheet of our Excel file. We have also selected only the rows in index 1, 3 and 5.

Reading Multiple Excel Sheets

We can read multiple Excel sheets with different data forms using the *read_excel* function and the *ExcelFile* wrapper class. Consider the following example in which we are reading the contents of the two sheets then displaying them on the Python terminal:

```python
import pandas as pd
with pd.ExcelFile('employees.xlsx') as xls:
    data1 = pd.read_excel(xls, 'Sheet1')
    data2 = pd.read_excel(xls, 'Sheet2')

print("****Result from Sheet 1****")
print (data1)
print("")
print("***Result from Sheet 2****")
print (data2)
```

The code will return the following upon execution:

```
****Result Sheet 1****
        id,surname,wage,start_date,dept
0         1,John,656.3,2014-03-02,Finance
1       2,Mercy,498.2,2015-08-21,Operations
2          3,Kogan,711,2014-11-15,ICT
3           4,Milly,729,2016-05-12,HR
4       5,Gary,856.21,2015-03-22,Finance
5           6,Pendo,578,2014-06-21,ICT
6    7,Michael,488.8,2014-07-28,Operations
7         8,Gerald,622.5,2013-06-16,HR

***Result Sheet 2****
   id     name  zipcode
0   1     john     3456
1   2    mercy     8976
2   3    kogan     5436
3   4    milly     8967
4   5     gary     9087
5   6    pendo     7823
6   7  michael     6734
7   8   gerald     4563
>>>
```

The above figure shows that the two sheets were read successfully.

However, we have selected all the contents of the two sheets. Sometimes, we may need to choose only some rows and columns when selecting the data. In such a case, we can use the *.loc()* method. The following code demonstrates how this can be done:

import pandas as pd
with pd.ExcelFile('employees.xlsx') as xls:
  data1 = pd.read_excel(xls, 'Sheet1')
  data2 = pd.read_excel(xls, 'Sheet2')

 # Using the multi-axes indexing method
print (data1)
print (data2.loc[[0,3,7],['zipcode']])

When executed, the code will return the following result:

```
         id,surname,wage,start_date,dept
0           1,John,656.3,2014-03-02,Finance
1        2,Mercy,498.2,2015-08-21,Operations
2              3,Kogan,711,2014-11-15,ICT
3               4,Milly,729,2016-05-12,HR
4         5,Gary,856.21,2015-03-22,Finance
5              6,Pendo,578,2014-06-21,ICT
6      7,Michael,488.8,2014-07-28,Operations
7            8,Gerald,622.5,2013-06-16,HR
   zipcode
0     3456
3     8967
7     4563
```

In the first sheet, that is, Sheet1, we have displayed all the contents of the file.

In the second sheet, that is, Sheet2, we have decided to display only the rows at index 0,3 and 7 and not for all columns, but only the *zipcode* column.

Chapter 7- Data Wrangling

This refers to the process data in various formats. It involves operations such as grouping, merging, concatenating etc. The data is analyzed and made ready for use with another set of data. Python provides us with various features that can be used for such operations.

Merging Data

The Pandas library has the *merge* function that can be used for joining data frame objects. Let us first create two data frames:

```
# import pandas library
import pandas as pd
df1 = pd.DataFrame({
     'id':[1,2,3,4,5],
     'Name': ['John', 'Milly', 'Gerald', 'Alex', 'Alice'],

'subject_id':['math','eng','phy','chem','bio']})
df2 = pd.DataFrame(
     {'id':[1,2,3,4,5],
     'Name': ['Felix', 'Grace', 'Benjamin', 'Joel', 'Eliza'],

'subject_id':['math','eng','phy','chem','bio']})
print(df1)
print(df2)
```

The code will return the following data frames when executed:

```
     Name   id  subject_id
0    John    1        math
1   Milly    2         eng
2  Gerald    3         phy
3    Alex    4        chem
4   Alice    5         bio
       Name   id  subject_id
0     Felix    1        math
1     Grace    2         eng
2  Benjamin    3         phy
3      Joel    4        chem
4     Eliza    5         bio
>>>
```

The *merge* takes the following syntax:

pd.merge(left, right, how='inner', on=None, left_on=None, right_on=None, left_index=False, right_index=False, sort=True)

The *merge* function serves as the base for all the standard join operations.

Grouping Data

Sometimes, we may need to calculate some measures based on groups of our data. There are various methods provided by the Pandas library that we can use to create groups from our data. Here is an example:

```python
# import pandas library
import pandas as pd

data = {'Team': ['Team1', 'Team1', 'Team2', 'Team2', 'Team3',
    'Team3', 'Team3', 'Team3', 'Team1', 'Team4', 'Team4', 'Team4'],
    'Rank': [1, 2, 2, 3, 3,4 ,1 ,1,2 , 4,1,2],
    'Year': [2014,2015,2014,2015,2014,2015,2016,2017,2016,2014,2015,2017],
    'Points':[784,746,863,684,742,798,644,788,682,703,804,691]}
df = pd.DataFrame(data)

grouped = df.groupby('Year')
print(grouped.get_group(2015))
```

What we have done is that the data have been grouped using the year, and then we have obtained the result for the specified year, which is 2015. The code will return the following when executed:

```
     Points  Rank   Team  Year
1       746     2  Team1  2015
3       684     3  Team2  2015
5       798     4  Team3  2015
10      804     1  Team4  2015
>>>
```

Data Concatenation

Pandas provides us with various ways to join our data. We can combine together DataFrame, Series and Panel objects. We can use the *concat* function for this purpose.

Let us create two data frames then concatenate them. Each data frame shows the best subject for each student:

```
# import pandas library
import pandas as pd
df1 = pd.DataFrame({
    'id':[1,2,3,4,5],
    'Name': ['John', 'Milly', 'Gerald', 'Alex', 'Alice'],
    'subject_id':['math','eng','phy','chem','bio']})
df2 = pd.DataFrame(
    {'id':[6,7,8,9,10],
    'Name': ['Felix', 'Grace', 'Benjamin', 'Joel', 'Eliza'],
    'subject_id':['geo','cre','bus','comp','agri']})

print(pd.concat([df1,df2]))
```

The two data frames will be created then merged. Execution of the code will generate the following:

```
      Name  id subject_id
0     John   1       math
1    Milly   2        eng
2   Gerald   3        phy
3     Alex   4       chem
4    Alice   5        bio
0    Felix   6        geo
1    Grace   7        cre
2 Benjamin   8        bus
3     Joel   9       comp
4    Eliza  10       agri
```

The contents of the two data frames have been concatenated.

Chapter 8- Measures of Central Tendency

The central tendency refers to a number of measures that help us understand how data is distributed. These measures can give us the average value for the dataset and help us know how wide the data is distributed.

The Pandas library provides us with a number of functions that can be used for calculation of a number of measures namely the mean, median and the mode. Let is discuss how these can be calculated:

Mean and Median

These values can be calculated easily for a dataset. This is demonstrated below:

import pandas as pd

#Creating a Dictionary of series

data = {'Name':pd.Series(['Tom','John','Naviya','Milly', 'Gerald', 'Alex', 'Alice','James','Ricky','Vin','Steve','Smith','Jack',

   'Chanchal','Gasper','Lee','Andres']),

```
'Marks':pd.Series([55,66,55,73,48,48,52,54,60,62,48,46]),

'Rating':pd.Series([4.23,3.24,3.98,2.56,3.20,4.6,3.8,3.78,2.98,4.80,4.10,3.65])}

#Creating a DataFrame
df = pd.DataFrame(data)
print("The Mean for the Distribution is:")
print(df.mean())
print("*******************************")
print("The Median for the Distribution is:")
print(df.median())
```

Mode

Your dataset may have the mode or it may not have. This will depend on whether the data is continuous or whether it has a value with maximum frequency. Remember that the mode is the value which has the maximum frequency in the dataset. The following code demonstrates how we can calculate the mode for a dataset with Pandas:

```
import pandas as pd

#Create a Dictionary of series
```

```
data = {'Name':pd.Series(['Tom','John','Naviya','Milly', 'Gerald', 'Alex',
'Alice','James','Ricky','Vin','Steve','Smith','Jack',

   'Chanchal','Gasper','Lee','Andres']),

'Marks':pd.Series([55,66,55,73,48,48,52,54,60,62,48,46])}
#Creating a DataFrame
df = pd.DataFrame(data)

print(df.mode())
```

The code should return the following:

```
     Marks      Name
0     48.0      Alex
1      NaN     Alice
2      NaN    Andres
3      NaN  Chanchal
4      NaN    Gasper
5      NaN    Gerald
6      NaN      Jack
7      NaN     James
8      NaN      John
9      NaN       Lee
10     NaN     Milly
11     NaN    Naviya
12     NaN     Ricky
13     NaN     Smith
14     NaN     Steve
15     NaN       Tom
16     NaN       Vin
```

This shows that the mode for the data is 48.

Chapter 9- Calculating Variance

Variance refers to the measure of how far a value is from the mean of the dataset. It is a good measure to show how the values are dispersed. It is normally measured by use of standard deviation. It can also be measured by use of skewness.

The Pandas library provides us with methods that can be used for calculation of these.

Calculating Standard Deviation

Standard deviation is simply the square root of variance. The Pandas library provides us with the *std()* method that can help us calculate the standard deviation for our dataset. This is demonstrated below:

import pandas as pd

#To create dictionary of series

data = {'Name':pd.Series(['Tom','John','Naviya','Milly', 'Gerald', 'Alex', 'Alice','James','Ricky','Vin','Steve','Smith','Jack',

   'Chanchal','Gasper','Lee','Andres']),

'Marks':pd.Series([55,66,55,73,48,48,52,54,60,62,48,46]),

'Rating':pd.Series([4.23,3.24,3.98,2.56,3.20,4.6,3.8,3.78,2.98,4.80,4.10,3.65])}

# To create a DataFrame
df = pd.DataFrame(data)

# To calculate the standard deviation
print(df.std())

The code will return the standard deviation for the dataset.

Calculating Skewness

This is a good measure to tell whether your data is symmetrical or skewed. If the value for index is between -1 and 1, the distribution is symmetric. If the value of index is less than -1, then your distribution is skewed to the left. If the value is not less than 1, the distribution is skewed to the right. The following code demonstrates how to calculate skewness of a dataset:

import pandas as pd

#Creating a Dictionary of series

```python
data = {'Name':pd.Series(['Tom','John','Naviya','Milly', 'Gerald', 'Alex',
'Alice','James','Ricky','Vin','Steve','Smith','Jack',
   'Chanchal','Gasper','Lee','Andres']),

'Marks':pd.Series([55,66,55,73,48,48,52,54,60,62,48,46]),

'Rating':pd.Series([4.23,3.24,3.98,2.56,3.20,4.6,3.8,3.78,2.98,4.80,4.10,3.65])}

# To create a DataFrame
df = pd.DataFrame(data)
print(df.skew())
```

Chapter 10- Normal Distribution

This type of distribution provides us with a way of presenting data by arranging the probability distribution of every value in the data. Majority of the values remain close to the mean, which results into a symmetric distribution.

There are various functions provided by the Numpy library that can be used for calculation of values for a normal distribution. We then generate histograms over which the probability distribution curve is plotted. Consider the example given below:

import matplotlib.pyplot as plt
import numpy as np

m, sigma = 0.5, 0.1
s = np.random.normal(m, sigma, 1000)

 # To create bins and histogram
count, bins, ignored = plt.hist(s, 20, normed=True)

 # To plot a distribution curve
plt.plot(bins, 1/(sigma * np.sqrt(2 * np.pi)) *

   np.exp(- (bins - m)**2 / (2 * sigma**2)), linewidth=3, color='y')

plt.show()

This will generate the distribution curve given below:

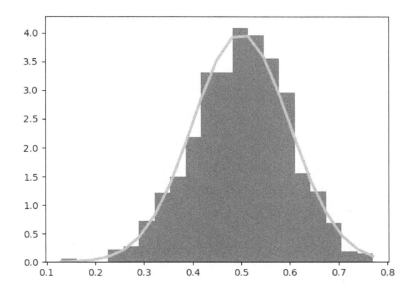

That is how a normal distribution should be.

Chapter 11- Working with JSON Data

JSON stands for JavaScript object notation and it stores data as text and in a human-readable format. Pandas has the *read_json* function that can be used for reading JSON data. A JSON file should be saved with a .json extension in the file name.

Let us begin by creating a JSON file. Copy the following code into notepad then save it with the name *employees.json*.

```
{
  "ID":["1","2","3","4","5","6","7","8" ],

  "Name":["Tom","John","Naviya","Milly", "Gerald", "Alex", "Alice","James"]

"Salary":["453.3","613.2","511","627","642.25","477","772.8","712.5" ],

  "StartDate":[
"1/1/2013","9/23/2012","11/15/2012","5/11/2016","3/27/2011","5/21/2013",
    "7/30/2013","6/17/2014"],

  "Dept":[
"IT","Operations","IT","HR","Finance","IT","Operations","Finance"]
}
```

Reading JSON Files

The *read_json* function provided by JSON helps us read JSON into a data frame. The following code demonstrates how to do this:

import pandas as pd
data = pd.read_json('employees.json')
print(data)

Selecting Specific Rows and Columns

We can also use the *read_json* method of Pandas to read only certain rows and columns from our JSON file. The multi-axes indexing method *.loc()* is used for locating the rows and columns that we specify. Let us demonstrate how this can be done:

import pandas as pd
data = pd.read_json('employees.json')

 # Use multi-axes indexing method
print(data.loc[[1,3,5],['salary','name']])

Chapter 12- Data Visualization

Data visualization is very important. It makes it easy for people to understand data. People easily understand graphics compared to text. Text becomes even more difficult to understand when it involves numerical data. With Pandas and Numpy libraries, you can easily visualize your data for ease of understanding. Let us discuss the various ways you can visualize your data using these two libraries:

Basic plotting

We can call the *plot()* function to visualize our data kept in a Series or data frame. This is demonstrated below:

```
import numpy as np
import matplotlib.pyplot as plt
import pandas as pd

df = pd.DataFrame(np.random.randn(10,4),index =pd.date_range('1/1/2010',

  periods=10), columns=list('ABCD'))

df.plot()
plt.show()
```

We have generated some random numbers into a Pandas data frame. We have then used this data to create plot. The *show()* method is defined in matplotlib and it helps us to display the plot. The code returns the plot given below:

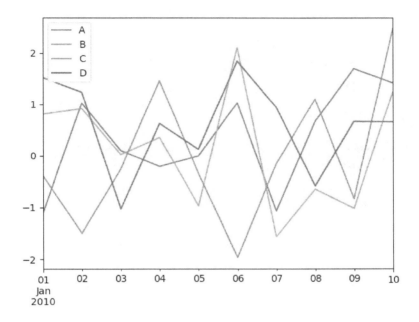

If the index has dates, it has to call *gct().autofmt_xdate()* so as to format the x-axis just as shown above. It is also possible for us to plot a column against another using keywords x and y.

The plotting methods provide us with other plot styles instead of the default plot style only. Due to this, we can create other types of plots as we are going to discuss below.

Bar plot

In Pandas, we can call the bar() method to help us create a bar plot. We will generate some random numbers and use them to create the plot as shown below:

```
import numpy as np
import matplotlib.pyplot as plt
import pandas as pd

data = pd.DataFrame(np.random.rand(10,4),columns=['a','b','c','d'])

data.plot.bar()
plt.show()
```

The code will generate the plot given below:

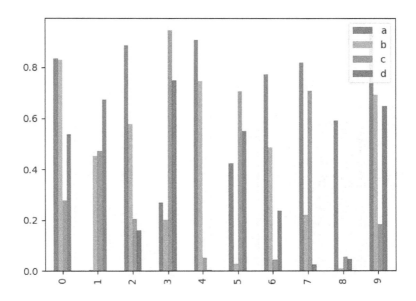

The plot is not stacked. However, we can still make it stacked by passed the parameter pass *stacked=True* to it as shown below:

import numpy as np
import matplotlib.pyplot as plt
import pandas as pd

data = pd.DataFrame(np.random.rand(10,4),columns=['a','b','c','d'])

data.plot.bar(stacked=True)
plt.show()

The code will generate s stacked plot as shown in the following figure:

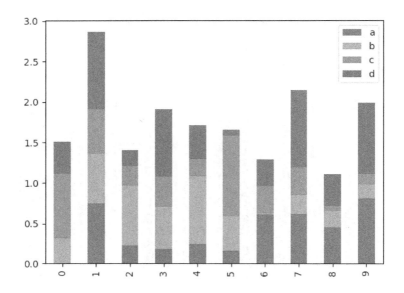

You have noticed that the bars in the two plots given above run vertically. Sometimes, you may prefer to have the bars run horizontally. This is possible. You only need to call the *barh* method, in which *h* if for *horizontal*. This should give you a plot with the bars running horizontally. Let us demonstrate this:

import numpy as np
import matplotlib.pyplot as plt
import pandas as pd

data = pd.DataFrame(np.random.rand(10,4),columns=['a','b','c','d'])

data.plot.barh(stacked=True)

plt.show()

The code will return the plot shown below:

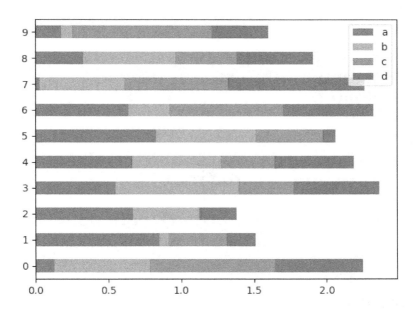

As shown, the bars are now running horizontally.

Histograms

To create an histogram from a dataset, we only have to call the *plot.hist()* method. We are allowed to specify the number of bins that we need to have as shown below:

```
import numpy as np
import matplotlib.pyplot as plt
import pandas as pd

data = pd.DataFrame({'a':np.random.randn(1000)+ 1,'b':np.random.randn(1000),'c':

np.random.randn(1000) - 1}, columns=['a', 'b', 'c'])

data.plot.hist(bins=16)
plt.show()
```

In the code given above, we have chosen to use 16 bins.

After execution, the code will generate the following plot:

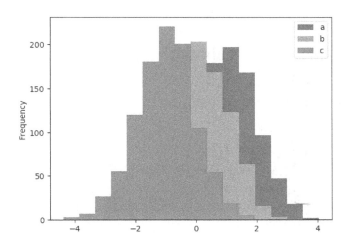

Sometimes, you may prefer to have each a histogram for each column. This is achievable with the code given below:

import numpy as np
import matplotlib.pyplot as plt
import pandas as pd

data=pd.DataFrame({'a':np.random.randn(1000)+1,'b':np.random.randn(1000),'c':

np.random.randn(1000) - 1}, columns=['a', 'b', 'c'])

data.diff.hist(bins=16)
plt.show()

Box Plots

This type of plot helps us show how the values are distributed in each column.

It can be created by calling the Series.box.plot() and DataFrame.box.plot(), or DataFrame.boxplot(). Consider the example given below:

```
import numpy as np
import matplotlib.pyplot as plt
import pandas as pd

data = pd.DataFrame(np.random.rand(10, 4), columns=['A', 'B', 'C', 'D'])

data.plot.box()

plt.show()
```

The code generates the box plot given below:

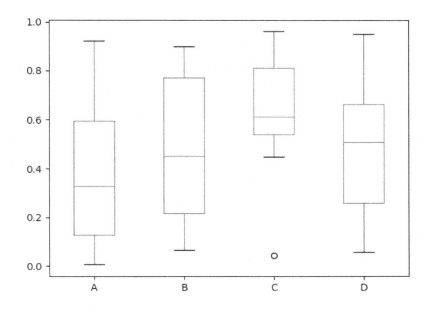

The box plot given above is for 4 trials in 10 observations of some uniform random variable on [0, 1].

Scatter Plot

A scatter plot normally shows many points plotted on a Cartesian plane. Each point is a representation of two variables. One of the variables is chosen from the vertical axis while the other one is chosen from the horizontal axis. To create a scatterplot in Pandas, we only have to call the DataFrame.plot.scatter() method. The following code demonstrates how to plot a scatterplot in Python:

```
import numpy as np
import matplotlib.pyplot as plt
import pandas as pd

data = pd.DataFrame(np.random.rand(50, 4), columns=['a', 'b', 'c', 'd'])

data.plot.scatter(x='a', y='b')

plt.show()
```

The code returns the following plot:

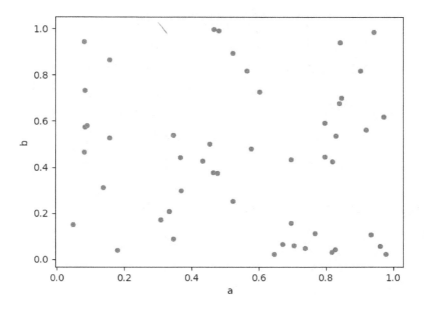

Each point is plotted to where it lies, that is, the point of intersection between its x and y variables. The data points were generated randomly.

Bubble Chart

Bubble charts normally display the data in the form of a cluster of circles. The data for creation of a bubble chart should have the xy coordinates, size and the color of the bubbles. The library is capable of supplying the colors. To create bubble charts in Pandas, we have to call the *DataFrame.plot.scatter()* method. This is demonstrated below:

```
import matplotlib.pyplot as plt
import numpy as np

# creating the data
x = np.random.rand(20)
y = np.random.rand(20)
z = np.random.rand(20)
colors = np.random.rand(20)
# Call the scatter function
plt.scatter(x, y, s=z*1000,c=colors)
plt.show()
```

The code will generate the chart given below:

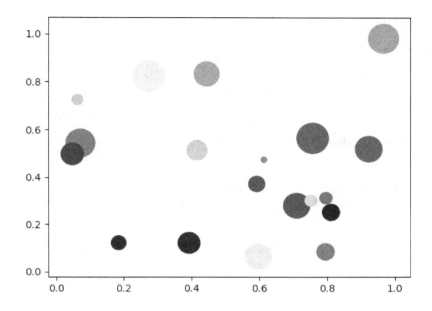

Heat Map

A heat map has values that represent various shades of same color for every value that is to be plotted. The darker shades of the chart normally represent higher values compared to the lighter shade. If the value is very different, you can use a completely different color. Consider the example given below:

```
from pandas import DataFrame
import matplotlib.pyplot as plt

data=[{1,3,4,2},{7,2,5,1},{5,3,1,2},{2,6,5,3},{1,9,2,6}]
Index= ['I1', 'I2','I3','I4','I5']
Cols = ['C1', 'C2', 'C3','C4']
df = DataFrame(data, index=Index, columns=Cols)

plt.pcolor(df)
plt.show()
```

The code will return the following plot:

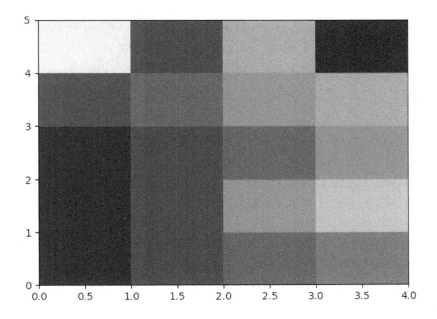

Area Plot

To create an area plot, we call the *Series.plot.area()* method. We can also call the *DataFrame.plot.area()* method and achieve the same result. The following code demonstrates how to create an area plot:

```
from pandas import DataFrame
import matplotlib.pyplot as plt
import pandas as pd
import numpy as np

data = pd.DataFrame(np.random.rand(50, 4), columns=['a', 'b', 'c', 'd'])

data.plot.area()

plt.pcolor(data)
plt.show()
```

The code generates the following plot:

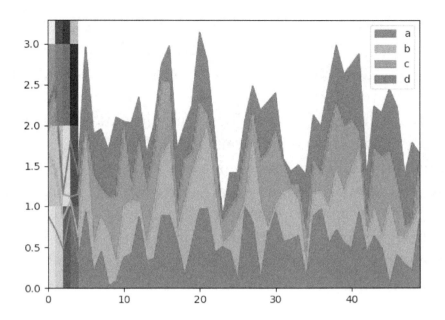

Conclusion

This marks the end of this guide. Data science is a very promising branch of artificial intelligence. It involves the creation of computing models that can extract intelligence from data. Companies generate data in huge amounts. This data is generated on a daily basis and kept in various storages, both online and offline. Processing of such data may be hard when approached manually. However, there are automated means through which we can extract intelligence from such data. Python is a programming language good for data science. It has a number of libraries that provide us with numerous functions for data analysis. Examples of such libraries are Numpy and Pandas. The two are libraries good for data science and Python supports them.

You only have to install these libraries on your system and begin to use them for data analysis. Python comes with a tool known as pip. The tool is installed automatically during the installation of Python. You can use this tool to install the two libraries on your system. There are also alternative ways of installing these libraries on your system. With Pandas, you can create a visual representation of your data for ease of understanding.

CPSIA information can be obtained
at www.ICGtesting.com
Printed in the USA
BVHW010750080819
555321BV00019B/87/P